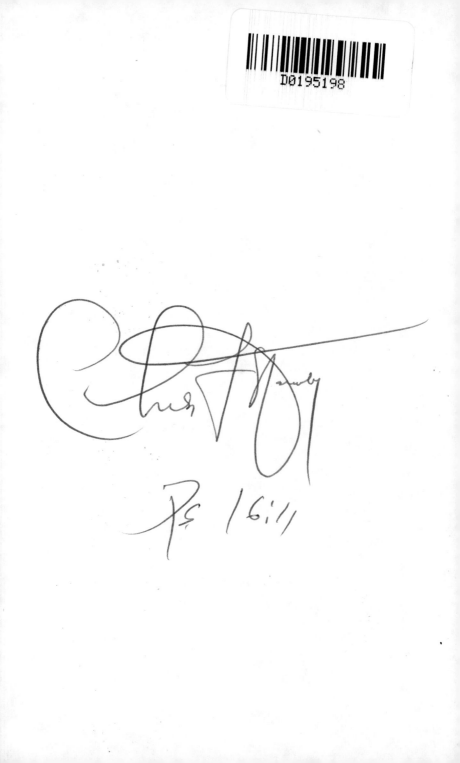

A Touch of His Goodness

Other Books in This Series

Meditations on God's Abundant Goodness

A Touch of His Goodness

with Original Photographs by

Charles Stanley

ZondervanPublishingHouse
Grand Rapids, Michigan

A Division of HarperCollins*Publishers*

A Touch of His Goodness
Copyright © 1998 by Charles F. Stanley

Requests for information should be addressed to:

📖 ZondervanPublishingHouse
Grand Rapids, Michigan 49530

Library of Congress Cataloging-in-Publication Data

Stanley, Charles F.
    A touch of his goodness : meditations on God's abundant goodness, with original photographs / by Charles F. Stanley.
       p.   cm.
    ISBN: 0-310-21489-0 (hardcover : alk. paper)
    [1. God—Goodness—Meditations.   2. Devotional calendars.]   I. Title.
BT137.S73 1998
231'.4—dc21   98-17451
                                                                       CIP

This edition printed on acid-free paper and meets the American National Standards Institute Z39.48 standard.

Printed in the United States of America

98 99 00 01 02 03 04 /❖ DC/ 10 9 8 7 6 5 4 3 2 1

Contents

Photographs

———— • ————

Introduction

Qo you believe that God is good? I do believe most Christians certainly at least mentally assent to the kindness and benevolence of God. Yet I sense that the goodness of God, while intellectually and doctrinally affirmed, is often questioned in the hearts of many Christians.

The culprit, I feel, is most frequently our routine encounters with adverse circumstances. We find ourselves in painful situations where there appears to be little evidence of God's goodness. We feel like victims of the indiscriminate, unfair, unjust, and evil actions of others. If God is so good, we mutter to ourselves, then why does all this happen to us?

When we lose sight of God's goodness, we are in grave danger of a drifting, inconsistent faith and diminishing joy. We can subtly nurture a grudge against God and find ourselves spiritually embittered. Once we understand, however, that God is intrinsically good in his being, nature, and acts toward us and incapable of doing anything but good, I believe we have the footing for an adventurous and enduring Christian experience.

The Bible is explicit (it always is) in its assertion of the incredible goodness of God. "Give thanks to the LORD, for he is good" (Psalm 107:1) is the unceasing refrain of the authors of Scripture. His benevolence and kindness to those who trust in him is unlimited. God has only our good in mind and his extraordinarily noble purposes for us can never be ultimately thwarted.

Here is the indispensable truth the Christian must embrace: even when our difficulties are overwhelming, our spirit wounded, our burdens heavy, *God is working everything together for good* (Romans 8:28). God never says our problems and their painful details are necessarily good in themselves. He does not ask us to deny the reality of evil and its myriad of harmful effects on our lives. What the Lord does tell us is that he mysteriously, wondrously weaves our anguish and ache into his good plan of making us into the image of Christ *because he is innately good.*

Each devotional in *A Touch of His Goodness* reflects the brilliant goodness of God and his expression of that goodness to the Christian. From creation to salvation to our eventual home in heaven, God's goodness is on triumphant display. The saint whose theology is firmly anchored in God's goodness will be encouraged and fortified for the stiffest of challenges and obstacles.

I trust you will accept the invitation of the psalmist to "taste and see that the LORD is good" (Psalm 34:8). As you do, you can experientially confess this hearty expectation of David: "I am still confident of this: I will see the goodness of the LORD in the land of the living" (Psalm 27:13).

A Touch of His Goodness

The LORD is my shepherd. I shall not be in want. . . .
Surely goodness and love will follow me all the days
of my life, and I will dwell in the house of the LORD forever.

PSALM 23:1, 6

The Goodness Pursuit

----------•----------

The Twenty-third Psalm, penned from the shepherd heart of David, is among the most beloved of any passage of Scripture. Many Christians memorized it during childhood and can accurately recite it throughout their life. Perhaps its appeal lies in its simplicity and the beautiful illustration of God's near and dear care of his people. It is not a passage that lends itself to thorough theological study, but even a slight investigation of the last verse reveals a major facet about the goodness of God.

When David composed the conclusion of this poem he knew well the richness of its meaning. "Surely goodness and love will follow me all the days of my life" (Psalm 23:6). This was not mere sentimental thought or a pleasant, cheerful way to end a heart-felt psalm. What David had in mind was an understanding and lavish presentation of God's goodness.

The Hebrew word for *follow* is most often translated "to chase or pursue." David used it several times in his writings, and almost invariably an unusual intensity accompanies its usage. The books of Samuel chose this word repeatedly to describe Saul's unrelenting hounding of David. So when David speaks of God's goodness following us throughout our lives, it literally means that God is actively pursuing us, chasing us down, with goodness. God is after you, never to condemn you, but to continually show just how good and merciful he is. God's goodness has a spiritual radar locked on your heart, and he is constantly releasing streams of blessings your way.

What an incredibly delightful way to think about God! All of my life, every day, in stress and ease, in work and play, in sickness and in health, God's goodness is unceasing. I spent too many years with an entirely different picture of God. I knew he was good, but I thought he dispensed his blessings in a far more measured manner. I could tap into his goodness on occasion, but the thought of God actually hunting me down with his benevolence was a completely alien concept. I had no idea that God loved me so much.

I know I am not alone in this thinking. I am afraid that most of us find this notion of God a bit unbelievable. I understand such reasoning, but the encouraging truth of God's Word is straightforward—God is so good that he has arranged immeasurable ways to express his goodness to you.

Let me suggest this mental and spiritual exercise to help transform your attitude about the goodness of God. Start your day with an affirmation that God is energetically pursuing you with his goodness. Restate this truth several times a day and continue for several weeks. You will build a new mindset that anticipates and recognizes the goodness of God. Practice this habit, especially in moments of tension and distress. You will find that God's goodness is never dissipated or negated by distressing circumstances and, even in the most painful hour, his goodness is intensely pursuing you to comfort and strengthen your inner being.

———— • ————

Father, it does seem incredible that you really are actively pursuing me in order to lavish your blessings with all their goodness and mercy heaped upon them. Plant this truth deep within my heart so that in times of despair I will not forget the magnitude of your love for me.

Touchstone

Stop pursuing

what is actually

trying to

catch you.

God saw all that he had made, and it was very good.

GENESIS 1:31

Don't Doubt

---•---

The goodness of God shimmers on the very first pages of Scripture. As God majestically composes the universe, he gazes at the work of his hands and declares it "good." Casting his pure eye over earth, sky, water, creatures, and Adam and Eve, God deemed his work "very good" (Genesis 1:31).

There in the garden of innocence, divine goodness was perfectly displayed. Adam and Eve and God lived in flawless union. The only utopia that ever existed—apart from heaven—was in seamless operation until the Tempter arrived. No one really knows how long Adam and Eve inhabited the unspoiled moral and temporal beauty of the Garden before they succumbed to sin, but we sense that it was not for long.

Although there are several suppositions as to why the duo was seduced by the Devil, there is clear evidence that part of the Deceiver's scheme was to shed doubt about God's goodness. That is the kernel of Satan's questioning to Eve: "Did God really say, 'You must not eat from any tree in the garden'?" (Genesis 3:1). The Devil started Eve on a spiritually truant and deadly path. Was God withholding something good from her? Did God's command to abstain from eating the fruit of one tree in the midst of the garden stem from a greedy nature? Was he stingy?

Satan was dead wrong, of course, but can you see how he operates in a similar manner today? God does promise to supply our needs; but when we experience lack, we wonder if he is really that good and able. We pursue ambitions or possessions that involve inordinate desires because we are dissatisfied with his blessings. Like the first couple, we are not quite sure God's instructions are for our complete welfare. Doubting his goodness, we search after something or someone that can make us feel better or look better to others.

Understand this: Behind every injunction, command, and exhortation of Scripture is the innate goodness of God. When God restricts us from certain behavior it isn't because he is opposed to our happiness but precisely because he delights in our well-being.

God knows the consequences of misdirected thoughts and deeds and in his goodness warns us not to participate in them. As we learn to accept God's kindness and wisdom as the premise for all his promises, precepts, and commands, then our motivation to obey is crystallized.

If you are wrestling with temptation in a particular area where God has posted clear warning signs, remember that the scriptural signage is placed by God's loving hand. He has created you to enjoy him and his creation in innumerable ways. "The lions may grow weak and hungry, but those who seek the LORD lack no good thing" (Psalm 34:10). God withholds from you only that which will harm you. Aren't you grateful?

---------- ❖ ----------

Lord Jesus, please forgive me for the many times that I doubted your provision in my life, for those times that I tried to control my own destiny, and for those times I succumbed to temptation. All the while you have been with me, involved in every detail, wanting only to draw me closer to you.

Touchstone

God is for us, not
against us.

Or do you show contempt for the riches of his kindness, tolerance and patience, not realizing that God's kindness leads you toward repentance?

ROMANS 2:4

An Uncommon Kindness

——— • ———

Repent and confess—not pleasant words, are they? More often than not, they seem to associate themselves with disagreeable events or emotions we would rather forget or ignore. They sound shrill, even in print. So how is it that the apostle Paul actually weaves the kindness of God into a theological context that has so many dark threads? Despite the plainly uncomfortable feelings that accompany repentance and confession of sin, the exercise of such spiritual discipline is pivotal to enjoying the blessings of God. Repentance and confession are not designed to be a shameful guilt trip, but precise instruments by which God shapes our lives and ushers in renewal and cleansing.

God uses the Holy Spirit to convict us of sin, not the critique of other Christians, or a rousing sermon—though he may use these agents to confront us with truth. Were it not for this special work of the Holy Spirit, no person could be saved or mature in his faith. Think of the consequences if the Holy Spirit did not point out to us specific areas of disobedience. How grateful we should be that God's Spirit spotlights our sin in a loving fashion so we can avoid the pitfalls of rebelling against God. The incredible goodness of God leads us to repent and confess our sin.

The Greek word for *repent* conveys the notion of "turning around and going in the other direction." There is great force behind its usage. When we repent and acknowledge our wrong, we escape the escalating consequence of continued sin. God realizes the attractiveness of the world and in his goodness provides repentance to keep us on a godly course. The word is found most frequently in conjunction with salvation. When we turn to Christ as Savior, we are repenting, or turning away, from a misguided, selfish life. The great news is that God's lovingkindness is continually orchestrating circumstances to draw us to repentance. We cannot turn to God apart from his goodness to reveal our need for Christ and his forgiveness.

Christians often view confession in the same light as repentance, but there is a difference. The Greek means "to agree with." When a Christian confesses his sin, he is quite literally agreeing with God that he has violated God's precepts. Confession restores the intimacy of fellowship between people and God and removes any feelings of tension and distance. The peace of Christ settles in our hearts when we confess our sin to him. Since we are forgiven of all our sins—past, present, and future—the moment we are saved, the issue is full communion with Christ.

Again, God's goodness allows us to experience the riches of friendship with Christ through confession of sin. And again, the ministry of the Holy Spirit aids us in targeting specific areas of our lives that are in disagreement with God's ways.

Christ is your Savior because he is good enough to lead you to repentance and faith. He is your best friend because he is kind enough to listen and to accept your confession of sin. Take advantage of God's goodness today to turn away from evil. Ask the Holy Spirit to reveal any aspect of your life that is contrary to his will, and thank him for his kindness in restoring your relationship with your heavenly Father.

———— • ————

Father God, please forgive me for my disobedience in the area of _____. I confess that it was wrong and not what you have in your plans for me. I come, clinging to your love and restoration. Thank you for making me whole again.

Touchstone

What can seem
so bad to us,
God can use
for such
good.

Taste and see that the LORD is good.

PSALM 34:8

God Is Good

"God is great, God is good...."

It may have been years since you recited this childhood prayer. But time has not allowed you to forget the simple words of "The Blessing." Packed into this pithy petition we once mechanically repeated, however, is ageless significance and meaning.

God is great. This I believe and know. He is majestic, holy, righteous, and, in all respects, awesome. I am stirred to worship and praise as I consider just how great he is and how privileged I am to have a personal relationship with such a mighty God, through his son Jesus Christ.

God is good. This too I do believe and know—just not as consistently or passionately. Of course, when I am out for a brisk walk on a cool morning and all my photographs have turned out splendidly or the doctor just gave me a clean bill of health the day before, I can really soak in God's goodness to me. I feel wonderful, things are going well, and the future is promising. *God is certainly good to me*, I'll think and smile as I stroll. "Thank you, God, for being so kind." However, when circumstances are not so pleasant and agreeable, God's goodness is not quite so prominent in my thinking. I complain. I grumble. And like anyone, I get into the annoying and frustrating business of asking, "Why, God?"

Fortunately, these times usually are not lengthy sieges, and, in time, God's grace underscores his goodness. Still, it is far easier to lose sight of God's goodness rather than his greatness.

Contrary circumstances can cause us to sometimes question God's benevolence. Yet God is no less good than he is great. His goodness is constant, unchanging, and unimpaired by our predicaments. As Stephen Charnock notes in his treatise *The Existence and Attributes of God*, "God always glitters with goodness as the sun . . . doth with light."

If you have struggled with nagging suspicions about God's goodness, or perplexing circumstances have raised bothersome questions, I encourage you to consider afresh the inexhaustible goodness of God. Join in the psalmist's invitation to "taste" of God's goodness, to personally partake of the Lord's lovingkindness. To talk about it or even think too much about it will not do; eventually you must come to experience it for yourself.

———— • ————

Dear God, it can be so much easier at times to see only your greatness. Help me to see you in all your goodness as well. As I continue to read and pray, point out to me all the goodness you want to demonstrate in and through my life.

Touchstone

Allow the light of
God's goodness
to shine
upon you.

I know, O LORD, that a man's life is not his own; it is
not for man to direct his steps.

JEREMIAH 10:23

The Good Will of God

---

*P*erhaps life has not worked out exactly as you had scripted. You have a vocation, but it's not in demand. You can think of other jobs you would enjoy much more than the one you have. Your family has managed to stay together, but you never thought there would be so many battles. Overall, you are just not as successful or happy as you had envisioned.

I want to encourage you to at least momentarily waive any trappings of disillusionment and consider the astounding certainty that God has from eternity constructed a good plan for you. He is always up to good in your life. The apostle Paul called this God's "good, pleasing and perfect will" (Romans 12:2). You may think your current situation is anything but good, pleasing, or perfect. In fact, it may be far from it; but if you allow God to reshape your thinking and living, you can break out of mediocre Christianity and discover just how good God really is.

God decisively pierced the clouds of doom and oppression that hung on the Hebrew captives in Babylon with this burst of divine encouragement to the afflicted prophet Jeremiah: "'For I know the plans I have for you,' declares the LORD, 'plans to prosper you and not to harm you, plans to give you hope and a future'" (Jeremiah 29:11). It is his word to you as well. However bleak your current condition, your past experiences, or your future outlook, God has a good plan for you. It can happen. It can work. You have great hope for tomorrow when you embrace the good news of God's skillful and compassionate design for your life.

God's gracious plan for you began before he created the world (Ephesians 1:4). Before time, space, or matter, God had you in his mind, providentially arranging and orchestrating your life. When you were saved by the grace of Christ, God's amazing plan of salvation was activated. "Being confident of this, that he who began a good work in you will carry it on to completion until the day of Christ Jesus" (Philippians 1:6). What God starts, he finishes; and he has pledged himself to sustain and help you every step of your spiritual journey. When you were saved, something fantastic happened. You were delivered from darkness to light, from death to life, from the dominion of Satan to God. And that is just the beginning. There's so much more to come—times of warm fellowship with him, answers to prayer, guidance for crucial decisions, discernment for opportunities.

The good will or plan of God is precisely what Jesus clung to as he endured persecution and faced the brutal reality of the cross. Jesus knew the Father had a supremely faithful plan for his life even though it included the horror of the crucifixion. God was reconciling the world to himself through the ageless plan of redemption.

The same Father has crafted a noble plan for you. It may cover some perplexing terrain, but it is the best possible plan you could conceive, perfectly designed by a loving God. He promises you eternal and abundant life (John 10:10), a life so rich and rewarding that it exceeds your wildest anticipation. All he asks is that you trust him moment by moment to execute his purposes while resisting feelings of despondency and despair. The Holy Spirit will renew your mind with the encouraging power of Scripture, and you will progressively come to know and experience the good, acceptable, and pleasant will of God—his best for you.

———— • ————

Jesus, help me now to relinquish my selfish desires for my life. I am not going down the road I had planned, but I don't know my tomorrows, you do. Help me to abide in your omniscient knowledge with your peace ever present.

Touchstone

No one relying

on God's direction

ever got lost on

the trail.

The secret things belong to the LORD our God .

The Secret Things

———— • ————

We are inquisitive folk. We like to be in the know. We boast of the advantages of living in an age where volumes of material can be accessed in a single computer stroke. In our quest for information and facts, we are sometimes confused as to why God does not unload his full data base for our lives in the same instantaneous manner we gather other information. Why does an all-knowing God who sees all our days before we are even born seemingly keep us in the dark when our need is urgent?

It is no more than the goodness of God that keeps the curtain tightly drawn on most facets of our existence. We are completely incompetent to handle a full revelation of his plan for us. When God called Moses in the forlorn desert wilderness to lead the Hebrews, Moses' lack of confidence was evident in his tenuous response (Exodus 3:11). What do you think would have happened if God had unfolded the specific conflicts and demands Moses would encounter during the next forty years? I have a feeling Moses would have put his sandals back on and retreated further into the desert.

God appointed David as King of Israel when he was a teenage shepherd, but he did not disclose the exhaustion and isolation he would experience due to King Saul's relentless persecution. How would David have reacted if he had known the next several years would be spent playing a deadly game of hide and seek with a demented tormentor? The apostle Paul was plainly informed of future suffering when dramatically saved

(Acts 9:16–18), but God did not relate the austere details of jail, beatings, stoning, and constant rejection by the Jews.

God fashioned us to face life one day at a time. In his goodness, he gives us grace and help for each day. Although we may have some notion of what lies ahead, it is up to God to faithfully fill in the blanks. We are not to worry about tomorrow, only to abide in Christ today, to pray for our "daily bread." God knows our frail frame and understands we can handle only so much. Daily we are to trust in his goodness and depend on him for the wisdom and strength we need. Don't fret that you don't know it all. You really don't want to, do you? That's God's job description, and he is the only one who can fulfill it. He will tell you what you need to know, when you need it.

———— • ————

Father, thank you that you, being our creator, know just what we can handle in life. Help me to remember this the next time I get impatient with you, wanting you to reveal something I have no need to really know. Your goodness applies to all of my life—the known and unknown.

Touchstone

All of our unknowns

God knows

very well.

For the Son of Man is going to come in his Father's glory with his angels, and then he will reward each person according to what he has done.

MATTHEW 16:27

Rewarded Living

————— • —————

Rewards are great motivation to learning and achieving. Business, industry, education, and numerous other segments of society know the magnetic power of positive rewards. Who doesn't appreciate a merit pay increase that reflects on productive work? Who isn't thankful for encouraging words that compliment our attitude or effort?

In his goodness, our heavenly Father has granted his children the godly incentive of rewarded living. No small deed of kindness is ever in vain when done unto Christ. No diligently completed task goes unnoticed. Every word and deed is duly noted by our omnipresent, all-caring Father and will be rewarded. "God is not unjust," said the author of the magnificent letter to the Hebrews. "He will not forget your work and the love you have shown him as you have helped his people and continue to help them" (Hebrews 6:10). Never give in to the despondency and despair of thinking your life doesn't count, that your contribution to the kingdom is insignificant. God is watching. God will reward you. He remembers all you do and say and eternally acknowledges and blesses your deeds and words of devotion and service.

The thrust of Scripture is future reward. All believers in Christ will be rewarded for their activity on earth when they appear before Christ (2 Corinthians 5:10; 1 Corinthians 3:10–15). The key is not the scope or magnitude of our work, but rather our basic motivation to please God (1 Corinthians 4:3). If your heart is bent toward God and you want his praise more than the approbation of men, then you are laying up rich rewards in heaven. When you look into Christ's eyes—and what a moment that will be—you can hear him say, "Well done" (Matthew 25:21).

Will not those two words alone be worth all the ingratitude and neglect that we endure now? Will not the gleam of love in his eye so overwhelm you with delight that every remembrance of injustice will be instantly erased? The rewards of the Father will be dispensed with unimaginable magnanimity and grace.

As appealing as God's future rewards are, he also promises a degree of recompense on earth. Obedience to Christ brings the very blessed reward of seeing God at work and experiencing his best. Speaking of God's laws and commands, the psalmist assures that "in keeping them there is great reward" (Psalm 19:11). When we do what God asks, we enjoy the beneficial consequences of our behavior. Obedience may be very difficult, but the outcome will have the blessings of Christ. It is not only right to obey, it is profitable. Give and it will be given to you. Sow and you will reap. Put God first, and he will take full responsibility for your life.

Never forget that God honors your trust. "And without faith it is impossible to please God, because anyone who comes to him must believe that he exists and that he rewards those who earnestly seek him" (Hebrews 11:6). When you don't know what to do, trust God. When the way is painful and dark, trust God. Just a tiny spark of faith can pave the way for tremendous blessing.

The rewards of heaven. The rewards of obedience. The rewards of faith.

It's worth it all.

———— • ————

Lord, show me today what you want me to do to further your kingdom. Bring to mind things that I am involved in that would hinder my productivity for you. It is not the promise of reward that motivates me, but service to your Son, Jesus Christ, that allows me to express my love for you.

Touchstone

There are no second-
or third-place
finishers in heaven,
only winners.

The LORD is good to all; he has compassion on all he has made.

PSALM 145:9

An Angry God?

———— • ————

common but treacherous obstacle for both the Christian and the unbeliever is the belief that God is angry with them. The follower of Christ who adopts this notion is seldom happy with himself or secure in his fellowship with the Savior. The unsaved person either has no desire to know such a God or feels he is unapproachable. However, this distorted view of God turns the true character of Christ on its head.

God's goodness is showered on all creation. The Christian and non-Christian who stroll down a powdered beach and listen to the soothing rhythm of waves lapping the shore both enjoy the beauty of God's handiwork. A flaming sunset is just as spectacular to the unsaved as the saved. Here is how the apostle Paul described the all-encompassing benevolence of God: "In the past, he let all nations go their own way. Yet he has not left himself without testimony: He has shown kindness by giving you rain from heaven and crops in their seasons; he provides you with plenty of food and fills your hearts with joy" (Acts 14:16–17). Does this sound like a vindictive, vengeful God?

The cross of Christ has satisfied the just wrath of God. God's anger against sin was spent when Christ was crucified on a Jewish hillside. The love of God for us was publicly displayed in the once-for-all sacrifice of his Son. God is not out to get anyone. He does not want all of humanity to live on a gigantic guilt trip. He loves all men and women.

The Christian need never worry that God is piqued at him. "Therefore, there is now no condemnation for those who are in Christ Jesus" (Romans 8:1). There is nothing you can do or say that will turn God's love sour. He is not edgy or cranky or irritated with you. He has forgiven you completely of past, present, and future sins. Does that surprise you? For many, I think it does because we think God is somewhat like us, and we certainly can lose our composure. But God cannot be compared to anyone. He transcends all we can think or imagine. The non-Christian need not be afraid to approach God. Although his justice requires him to ultimately punish those who reject his offer of reconciliation, God is not angry with the unsaved person. Quite the contrary; he works unceasingly to help people understand his extraordinary offer of redemption through faith in Christ.

There is no scowl on the face of God. His eyes sparkle with divine delight at the possibility of bringing you into his happy family of children of faith in Jesus Christ.

———— • ————

Lord, I come, falling at your feet to accept the love you have for me. I've denied myself your love and goodness for so long because of a distorted view of you. Help me to remember that each day you wait to show me your love, not to hand out your wrath.

Touchstone

God's love knows no
earthly limits.

Godliness with contentment is great gain.

1 TIMOTHY 6:6

The Contented Life

————— • —————

We live in an age of discontent. It is hard to be satisfied with what we have when there is so much more we can obtain. Our culture incessantly tells us just how much more we can accumulate and how much better we will feel when we get it. Stroll into your local mall and you are instantly aware of the incredible number of things you can't purchase. Thanks to the persuasiveness of advertising and marketing, it's not about keeping up with the next-door Joneses any longer; it's about keeping up with all the Joneses all over the world. In *The Art of Divine Contentment*, Thomas Watson comments that "discontent is a fretting humour, which dries the brains, wastes the spirits, corrodes and eats out the comfort of life."

Still, discontent is not simply a modern-day problem. The toxic spiritual and emotional effects of envy and jealousy have plagued every culture. And it doesn't simply revolve around material possessions. There are people who really do appear to have it all materially but ache and throb with discontent inwardly. What they and we need is godly contentment. By this I do not infer passivity, resignation, or feathers never ruffled, but a soul that finds its ultimate peace and security in relationship to a good God. Jeremiah Burroughs in *The Rare Jewel of Christian Contentment* says, "Christian contentment is that sweet, inward, quiet, gracious frame of spirit, which freely submits to and delights in God's wise and fatherly disposal in every condition."

The contented Christian is one who truly believes that God provides all his needs. Jesus told the folks who gathered to hear one of his sermons that if he could adorn lilies with beauty and supply every bird of the air with food, he assuredly could take care of their basic requirements. Why worry and linger in discontent if God promises to route his inexhaustible resources to our precise need? Speaking to an audience at Wheaton College, Dr. J. I. Packer astutely said that contentment "is a matter of accepting from God's hand what he sends because we know that he is good and therefore it is good." You may not have the best wardrobe, the nicest car, the most striking home, or the most rewarding job; but for now this is God's provision. It may change, and God is certainly not opposed to progress, but you can rest content that God's hand is providing for the present.

The Christian who is free from the perpetual lust of discontent finds his greatest satisfaction in Christ. He realizes that more money, prestige, or power will not break the grip of covetousness, but that Christ alone satisfies. He loosens his hold on possessions, acknowledging that God is the source and owner of all. He entrusts his future to a sovereign God who commands us to "be content with what you have" because he will never abandon him (Hebrews 13:5). When you have Christ, you have all you will ever need, for now and eternity.

Before I gave my life to you, Father, I searched for that inner peace and contentment in the strangest of ways. Since Jesus came into my heart, that empty space is gone. It is now filled with your love.

Touchstone

Real contentment
comes from those
things we can
never lose.

He did not waver through unbelief regarding the promise of God.

ROMANS 4:20

Don't Stagger

———— • ————

If God visited you in an extraordinary manner and told you that he would be your divine protector and benefactor, wouldn't you be exhilarated? God did speak to Abram in a vision and pledged his blessings to the adventurous and obedient patriarch. "Do not be afraid, Abram. I am your shield, your very great reward" (Genesis 15:1). God reconfirmed what we term the Abrahamic Covenant, promising the aged Abram a son whose seed would number more than the "stars of the heaven." With no bright city lights to obscure Abram's vision, he could glance upward into the dark Middle East night and see thousands of white, shining stars. I imagine he probably looked for a moment to try to fathom exactly what God was promising. Here was a man whose likelihood of having one child, much less becoming a father of nations, was virtually nil. So what was his reaction to God's seemingly implausible promise? "Abram believed the LORD, and he credited it to him as righteousness" (Genesis 15:6).

God did more than Abram could possibly imagine. He made him the father of faith, reckoning God's righteousness to him and all after him who look to Christ, not their works, for salvation. Abram could never have envisioned the incredible legacy God had in store. Surely he did not comprehend God's full majestic purposes when the Lord first spoke to him in Haran (Genesis 12:1). Abram wanted a son through whom his name and inheritance could be perpetuated. God had something far grander in mind, bringing the blessings of saving faith to every generation after Abram. God even changed his name from Abram, "exalted father," to Abraham, "father of many."

God is willing to do immensely more than we can imagine. We ask sometimes for little when God is ready to do so much more. Paul described God's transcendent greatness in this way: "Now to him who is able to do immeasurably more than all we ask or imagine, according to his power that is at work within us" (Ephesians 3:20). How much is God willing to do for us? "Immeasurably" more. You can't limit the superabundant power of Christ at work in you and on your behalf. If you were to write down all of your fondest hopes and dreams for your life, that isn't even the starting point for God.

Could David the shepherd ever think he would be king? Could Gideon, a plain man, ever conceive he would be a mighty solider? Could fishermen like Peter and John ever anticipate they would catch souls instead of fish?

Are you expecting God to do great things in your life, or have you settled for a complacent faith? Never feel cornered by circumstances. Don't think for a moment that your life can never rise above the ordinary. You may live and work in the common round, but if you are willing to trust God, he can mark your life with his imprint. Ask him to have his way with you. Take him at his Word as you read Scripture. Don't tolerate unbelief. Focus on the unlimited greatness and goodness of God to make your life count in ways you can't begin to dream about. Tell God your most pressing need and then trust him to meet it in the most surprising and surpassing manner.

———— • ————

You are truly a great Father. Lord. Your plans for me are great. Help me make your plans a reality in my life by looking at my circumstances through your Word.

Touchstone

Aren't you glad
God is not limited
by your own
imagination?

He guides the humble in what is right and teaches them his way.

PSALM 25:9

A Big Impression

God is not easily impressed. In fact, the more I think about it, how exactly do you impress perfect, unflawed deity? My wisdom is comical measured against the omniscience of Christ. My skills are infantile when I think of the vast creative and sustaining power of God. I have to conclude then that trying to impress God is simply a waste of time. I cannot give enough money, serve enough people, attend enough Bible studies or worship services, memorize enough Scripture, or even obey enough biblical principles to sway God in any manner.

But there is one virtue revealed in the Scriptures that apparently does influence our awesome God. It is a key to answered prayer. It is a powerful determinant as to who God uses in the work of his kingdom. And who doesn't want prayers answered or to be part of God's selective service? The singular human attribute that God rewards is a humble heart and mind. Isaiah the prophet attached God's significance to humility when he declared the word of the Lord: "This is the one I esteem: he who is humble and contrite in spirit, and trembles at my word" (Isaiah 66:2). God is not looking for men and women who possess superior intelligence, affluence, or acumen. He is searching for those rare Christians who think majestically of Christ and never more highly of themselves than they should.

When God tapped Moses as the chief operating officer for the several million enslaved Hebrews of Egypt, Moses quivered with fear and offered nothing but excuses. "Who am I, that I should go to Pharaoh and bring the Israelites out of Egypt? . . . What if they do not believe me or listen to me? . . . I am slow of speech and tongue.... O Lord, please send someone else to do it" (Exodus 3:11; 4:1, 10, 13). Obviously, Moses didn't think he had the right resumé. So why did God choose him? When it came to humility, relying completely on God and not self, Moses was the clear choice for the Father.

When God sought a king to unite and lead a divided Israelite kingdom, he picked the youngest and rawest young lad of Jesse's household for the task. "The LORD does not look at the things man looks at. Man looks at the outward appearance, but the LORD looks at the heart," God told Samuel as he summoned Jesse's sons (1 Samuel 16:7). The man after God's heart and the one with a humble spirit was the shepherd boy we know as David.

If you are trying to impress God, quit. It's futile. If you really want him to anoint you with his favor and use you for his work, then humble yourself before the Lord by recognizing his power and admitting your inadequacy. You don't have to demean yourself, just realize that God's power flows to the weakest of saints, for they lean the heaviest on him. The more you humble yourself, the more grace God will give you, doing for you what you could never do on your own. If you need guidance, then humility is the highway (Psalm 25:9). If you want to lead an honorable life, then seek humility first (Proverbs 15:33). Let the finest piece of your spiritual wardrobe be humility (1 Peter 5:5).

———— • ————

Father, forgive me for the times I've been haughty or proud. I want nothing to come between me and my fellowship with Jesus. Teach me humility and help me to walk in it.

Touchstone

Boast only in
Jesus Christ.

There is no one righteous, not even one; ... there is
no one who does good, not even one.

ROMANS 3:10, 12

Not Good Enough

———— • ————

The prosperous young man came to Jesus with a pointed question: "Good teacher, what must I do to inherit eternal life?" (Luke 18:18). He held to the supposition, as the vast majority do today, that he could certainly be good enough or do enough good things to gain everlasting life. He should be commended for his discernment that there was more to life than work, pleasure, entertainment, and accomplishment. He somehow instinctively knew that he was meant for far nobler purposes. His mistake was the common misconception that afflicts today's seeker—that we must "do" something to earn salvation. The rationale is appealing. We are usually rewarded in this life according to effort. The greater the labor, the greater the reward. Surely this is how it must work in the spiritual realm as well, right?

Wrong. The first thing that Jesus did was to turn the man's notion of good on its head. "'Why do you call me good?' Jesus answered. 'No one is good—except God alone'" (v. 19). Jesus was certainly doing good things—healing, casting out tormenting spirits, preaching liberation from the complex laws of the Pharisees. However, he was doing them because he was God, not an extraordinary teacher or rabbi as the young man imagined. Jesus' definition of good was himself—that perfect standard to which no one could attain through self-effort. There are many very good men and women as we define good, but they can never be good enough to attain to the flawless righteousness of God. "There is no one righteous [good enough], not even one," Paul quoted the psalmist in his letter to the Romans (3:10). Eternal life is a gift from God that we cannot procure through good works. God alone is good and bestows his goodness to those who realize they cannot measure up to God's standards and who receive the gift of salvation through faith in Christ.

C. S. Lewis described the plight of all who seek to be good in God's sight in *C. S. Lewis: Readings for Meditation and Reflection.* "All right, Christianity will do you good, a great deal more good than you ever wanted or expected. And the first bit of good it will do you is to hammer into your head (you won't enjoy that!) the fact that what you have hitherto called 'good'—all that about leading a decent life and 'being kind'—isn't quite the magnificent and all-important affair you supposed. It will teach you that in fact you can't be 'good' (not for twenty-four hours) on your own moral effort. And then it will teach you even if we were, you still wouldn't have achieved the purpose for which you were created. Mere morality is not the end of life. You were made for something quite different from that.... The people who keep on asking if they can't lead a decent life without Christ don't know what life is about."

We can't make it to heaven or know God even when we consistently put our best foot forward. We are depraved people, incapable of relating to God apart from faith in Christ's death, burial, and resurrection. We certainly can inherit eternal life, but only through faith in Christ's effort on the cross, not ours.

———— • ————

Lord Jesus, I've been working myself to death to get to you. Now I know I don't have to put forth one ounce of strength; I only need to cry out to you—the Son of God—who died on a cross for me. You endured the pain of all my sins and rose victoriously, fully alive once again. I accept your finished work and your offer of salvation now.

Touchstone

Our best foot
forward is the
step we make
toward the
cross.

As the heavens are higher than the earth, so are my ways higher than your ways and my thoughts than your thoughts.

ISAIAH 55:9

A Good Understanding

---•---

twelve-year-old boy strolls casually into his fifth grade math class. He sits nonchalantly at his desk until a balding, mustached teacher quietly comes to the front of the class. The teacher is Albert Einstein, and he announces he will explain the famous formula for mass and energy conversion. The chalk squeaks across the blackboard, and the young lad stares blankly at Einstein's diagrams. The student, along with the entire class, is dumbfounded. Mr. Einstein is from another planet as far as they are concerned.

Once saved, we are launched on a great adventure of learning about God. We are indwelt by the infinite presence of God, and the mind of Christ is resident within. This could cause some rather serious problems. "'For my thoughts are not your thoughts, neither are your ways my ways,' declares the LORD" (Isaiah 55:8). Thankfully, God condescends to our level of spiritual comprehension to instruct us. We, like the young boy, are incompetent to fathom the mysteries of our divine teacher. He patiently and lovingly reveals himself to simpletons like us, never lording his unrestricted deity over our frail humanity.

His principal teaching aids are the Scriptures and the Holy Spirit. They are the "dynamic duo" through which God reveals himself and illumines his path. Think of it: The Spirit of God uses the Word of God to teach a twelve-year-old boy or an eighty-year-old woman about himself. He has communicated in an intelligible manner what we could find only incomprehensible apart from his divine initiative. He comes beside us, whatever our spiritual state or bearing, and offers to show us his way.

God helps us to understand his will. "Therefore do not be foolish, but understand what the Lord's will is" (Ephesians 5:17). We can do the will of God, his plans and purposes for the parts and sum of our life, because we can know it. We, of course, do not know all of it at once, but he will reveal what we need to know in order to obey for the moment. We can also understand his ways, how he works to accomplish his will. Some of his ways can be observed through his dealings with characters in Scripture. For instance, the life of Joseph in the Old Testament underscores God's desire for us to excel in our work and maintain a grateful attitude in even oppressive situations. The hotheaded apostle Peter shows us the appropriate balance between admirable enthusiasm and recklessness. The pinnacle of God's instructive goodness, however, is his eagerness to help us learn about him (Matthew 11:29). We sit at the feet of Jesus, and he draws us in as his friends and followers. We come to know Jesus in an intimate fashion. We, the creatures, are drawn into unending fellowship with our Creator. He lavishes on us the "Spirit of wisdom and revelation, so that [we] may know him better" (Ephesians 1:17).

God knows it all, but he does not act like a know-it-all. He stoops down to our crude desks of learning, looks lovingly into our eyes, and whispers in our hearts what we long and need to hear.

———— • ————

Heavenly Father, I come to you now, claiming your word that you can bestow on me your Spirit of wisdom and revelation, so I may know you better. I pray that the eyes of my heart be enlightened so I may know the hope you have called me to. Amen. (Ephesians 1:17, 18)

Touchstone

With God as

our teacher,

we cannot

fail.

For no matter how many promises God has made,
they are "Yes" in Christ.

2 CORINTHIANS 1:20

Promises, Promises

---◆---

God is a promise maker and keeper. The Scriptures teem with promises God has gleefully made and pledged to fulfill for his children. Some promises from the Father are coupled with our obedience. God will personally respond to our petitions *if* our requests align with his purposes (1 John 5:14–15). Personal and corporate revival can occur *if* we humbly acknowledge our sins (2 Chronicles 7:14). God has his reasons when he places stipulations on his promises, but there are thousands of Scripture promises that God simply states without reservation. He will provide for our needs (Philippians 4:19). He will always be with us (Matthew 28:20). He will give us strength and courage to face adversity (Isaiah 41:10). The staggering truth about a promise from God is that he guarantees its performance. "Not one of all the LORD's good promises to the house of Israel failed; every one was fulfilled," Joshua reminded his troops (Joshua 21:45).

God, of course, is under no obligation to confer such grand spiritual wealth to us. His grace, however, finds great satisfaction and happiness in granting his children "his very great and precious promises" (2 Peter 1:4). God pledges himself to act on our behalf because he rejoices in us. Our most special promises are made to those whom we love the dearest. So it is with the Father. We may have heard that angels in heaven are jubilant when one lost person is found by the Savior, but do you know God merrily hums and sings about each of his children (Zephaniah 3:17)? Picture God cheerfully celebrating over his relationship with you every day and taking such great delight in your fellowship that he can't wait to see you claim one of his promises. Heaven is simply an eternal love affair between the lover of our soul and the beloved. God's promises express the great pleasure he has in his people.

God shares his promises with us too so that we may trust him. As we are the apple of his eye, so he desires to be our chief delight. He wants us to look to him to supply our needs because he knows the more we trust him, the more we will love and enjoy him. We honor God when we trust him. Trusting God to fulfill his promises tells him that we consider him faithful. When God told Abraham he would have a son, Abraham "did not waver through unbelief regarding the promise of God, but was strengthened in his faith and gave glory to God, being fully persuaded that God had power to do what he had promised" (Romans 4:20–21).

God gives you exciting promises to prove and test. He does so for no other reason than he loves you and is eager to see you place your trust in him. Find a promise in Scripture that relates to a specific need you have right now. Look to God, not another person or any other resources, for the answer. I can say with all certainty that God will keep his Word. The goodness of God flows swiftly and abundantly through his refreshing promises. They are a sure and pure channel of blessing.

———— • ————

Father, I have never considered that you actually sing for joy over me personally. Help me realize the love and care you give me so I may hold tight to the promises you have made for me. I love you, Lord.

Touchstone

God's track

record on

promises is

perfect.

I lift up my eyes to the hills—where does my help come from? My help comes from the LORD, the Maker of heaven and earth.

PSALM 121:1–2

God Sees

———— • ————

The tenet that God sees the believer's life in its entirety is disconcerting to some. They do not linger long on this topic because it entails God's unobstructed view of their sins and indiscretions. This thinking is haplessly warped. God does not sit in judgment over our sins; we are thoroughly and eternally forgiven through Christ's sacrificial death. Actually, the soul-penetrating gaze of Christ is breathtakingly comforting and consoling. David's recognition of God's constant care (Psalm 121) is reassuring for Christians who may wonder about or doubt God's active, personal care in their lives.

Such intimate involvement is beautifully illustrated in Hagar's encounter with God. When Sarah mistreated the pregnant servant girl, Hagar fled into the desert—a human speck in the vast sand and stone of the Middle East. God spoke to her and promised that her offspring would be blessed. She described the encounter by exclaiming, "You are the God who sees me" from which a compound name of God—El-Roi—is derived (Genesis 16:13). It means the "God who really sees." Later Sarah's jealously again drove Hagar and her teenage son, Ishmael, from Abraham's tent. Their water gone and the desert heat blistering, she lay Ishmael down to die in the shade of a bush. She and the boy cried. God saw the tears running down their cheeks. "God heard the boy crying" (Genesis 21:17) is Scripture's narrative. The whimper of a teenager and his tears did not escape the all-seeing eye of God who revived the pair and again affirmed his providential purposes.

How big is a tear drop in an ocean of sand? How loud is a dying whimper in a clamoring universe? Big enough and loud enough for the God who sees to take notice and come quickly to their rescue.

God sees your tears. They may be tears of regret, guilt, shame, loneliness, or pain. No matter if you shed them silently or with great outcry, God sees them. As the One who will wipe away all our tears one day, he compassionately comforts us. He sees and hears our cries of grief and heartache, promising to heal "the brokenhearted" and soothe our wounds (Psalm 147:3).

You are not abandoned. You are not alone in the world. God sees and God cares. He watches over every intimate detail of your existence so he might minister to your most pressing needs. When no one else notices or seems to care, God is your dearest friend. Allow him to speak to your spirit, calm your fears, and quiet your confusion. Feel his eternal grasp uplift you and support you as you find his grace sufficient and his love unfailing. Let the "God of all comfort" embrace you and keep you going with the sure knowledge that he sees your troubles, hears your pleas, and comes tenderly to your side.

———— • ————

I just want to stop and praise you now for thinking of me so dearly, for loving me through all my wrongdoings, and for caring for me like no other. There have been times in my life when I feel like Hagar must have felt in the desert, and you quenched my thirst and restored me. Thank you, Father.

Touchstone

The God who
really sees
really cares.

He who began a good work in you will carry it on to
completion until the day of Christ Jesus.

PHILIPPIANS 1:6

From Start to Finish

We can try so to succeed at the Christian life that we sometimes fail. We become so focused on our efforts to grow spiritually, we lose sight of God's role. We try to be like Christ; but the harder we try, the more frustrated we become. This scenario can quickly lead to repeated failure and frustration. If you have been snared in this messy process, the good news is that God has a way out.

You can be confident that what God begins he will finish. He didn't save you to let you flounder in uncertainty and anxiety. He has brought you into his family to experience an authentic, abundant life. The sagging Christian, weary of trying or plagued with guilt and regret over failure, can take great encouragement in God's plain promise to continue his work in you and present you spotless and blameless before the Father. There is no sin he has not forgiven. There is no failure that thwarts his love or plan for you. "It is God who works in you to will and to act according to his good purpose" (Philippians 2:13). God never gives up on you, so you never have to give up on yourself. He unceasingly, through good and bad, labors in you to accomplish his desire for you. The emphasis lies on "God works." There is nothing too difficult for him. He can clean up any mess you've made and enable you to move to spiritual maturity, wholeness, and happiness.

What is the work that God has begun? Clearly, he initiated the work of salvation. It isn't that you "got saved" but that "God saved you." Apart from his working, you could never know him. We love him only because he first loved us. At the moment of salvation, God began the work of sanctification, a lifelong process of developing you into Christlikeness. You can be holy only because God makes you holy. The task of sanctification is also the primary domain of God. Paul contested the Galatians' flawed reliance on the law—working to please God through self-effort—with this biting exhortation: "Are you so foolish? After beginning with the Spirit, are you now trying to attain your goal by human effort?" (Galatians 3:3). God works in you through the supernatural person of the Holy Spirit. The Spirit of God regenerated you in the new birth, and the same Spirit sanctifies you, revealing sin and empowering you to conquer its power. The Holy Spirit is your power source for Christian living. There is no other way.

God also began and will complete your faith. "Let us fix our eyes on Jesus, the author and perfecter of our faith" (Hebrews 12:2). When you feel like you have no faith or little faith, remember that God promises to perfect your faith. A fixed focus of faith on the power and might of Jesus Christ will sustain you as you deal with struggles and perplexities.

God is at work right now to achieve his good and kind purposes. He will finish the job. Count on him.

———— • ————

Thank you, Father, that you are the one working; you are not waiting on me to improve myself. I truly desire to be like Jesus and I know you want that for me, too. I am going to rest in your ability to see me through and wait with great expectation of all that you will accomplish through me.

Touchstone

Christ did not
save you in order
to abandon you.

In this world you will have trouble. But take heart! I
have overcome the world.

JOHN 16:33

In the Eye of the Storm

———— • ————

The storms of life can approach from any direction. They can ride the red winds of financial distress. They can blow in on angry words and remarks of a relational dispute. They can gather ominously on the horizon of a physician's bleak diagnosis. When Jesus put the finishing touch on his magnificent Sermon on the Mount, he concluded with the analogy of homes built on sand and stone. It wasn't a matter of *if* the storms would come, but *when* they would come. I used to think that when I reached a certain age or level of spiritual maturity that the storms would subside or at least diminish in intensity. I was wrong. Trials still huff and puff and try very hard to blow my house of faith down. I cannot tell you how many times I have prayed something like this: "Lord, you have to get me out of this. If you don't, I really am not sure I can make it." Occasionally, the Lord, knowing my frame, does still the waves of woe that seem ready to submerge me. For these instances I am grateful. But this is not the norm. Most often the storms pound me spiritually and emotionally until God sees fit to bring relief.

It has taken a long time, but I have learned a valuable lesson: *When God does not choose to calm the storm without, he is faithful to calm the storm within.* I actually think this the normative way of God. We inhabit a thorny universe filled with evil and turmoil. God has put us into this world and assured us that tribulation would be our common experience (John 16:33). Whirlwinds of adversity aren't the exception, they are the rule; and God has built us to withstand the surges of despair, abandonment, and disappointment by reinforcing us from within. The peace of God that he deposits in the deep reservoir of our spirit can sustain us in our darkest hour. The peace of Christ is that supernatural calm and contentment that completely contradicts the intensity of our struggle. It frequently flies in the face of reason and circumstance. The cancer eats away more of our bones, but our peace remains. The economic uncertainty of our job grows more unstable by the day, but the peace of God keeps us steady.

The peace of God comes from knowing he is in charge. We are not pawns to disease or the economy or the personal whims of another, but disciples of the sovereign God whose rule is over all. We cannot be victimized if we belong to the Victor, the one who is the Overcomer of all that opposes or threatens to undo us. The peace of God comes from abandonment to Christ. We belong to him. We are in his care. He is our sun and shield, our protector. God assumes total responsibility for the person who is completely committed to him. We have given the matter to God to solve. He is able. He is loving. He is wise. If he does not elect to stop the winds, then we know that he is walking with us through them, step by step, thought by thought, day by day.

Christ himself is your peace. Whatever may be wreaking havoc in your life can be faced with the placid assurance that Jesus Christ, the Lord of peace, is resident within. Turn to him. Trust him. Accept his peace for your anxiety. You will not fall apart or crumble, for the peace of God sustains and strengthens you. A noted writer once said, "What lies before you and behind you is nothing compared to what lies within you."

Jesus Christ is within you. Right now and forever.

———— • ————

I am enduring my own personal storm right now. You know what it is, Lord Jesus. It is hard for me to see my tomorrows very clearly. I fall down at your feet right now, giving you my all, seeking in you refuge from the winds.

Touchstone

The bigger the
storm, the more
reason to cling
to the anchor
of our faith.

Let your gentleness be evident to all.

PHILIPPIANS 4:5

God's Disposition

———— • ————

hat is God's disposition? Attributes such as love, grace, and mercy are often and accurately used to describe God's nature. Jesus used several definitive "I am" declarations in the book of John to describe his divine personhood and purpose. While these certainly tell us much about the Savior, Jesus tells us the surprising kernel of his disposition in this well-known invitation: "Come to me, all you who are weary and burdened, and I will give you rest. Take my yoke upon you and learn from me, *for I am gentle and humble in heart*" (Matthew 11:28–29, emphasis mine). Jesus is the gentle Savior. Jesus is gentle and humble. The Lion of Judah is also the Lamb that was slain. The King of Kings is a tender Shepherd of frail sheep.

God's presence and voice came to an exhausted Elijah in a "gentle whisper," not in the thunderous roar of earthquake, hurricane, and fire. The awesome God who had split rocks and parted seas came to Elijah on a gentle breeze, soft but still rich enough with holy majesty that Elijah reverently wrapped his cloak across his face as God spoke to him (1 Kings 19:11–13). When you feel discouraged or depressed as Elijah was, isn't it the gentle voice of Christ that you long to hear? God comes to us as a gentleman. He doesn't shout. Our soul and mind need to be uncluttered and stilled so we can hear him.

A spirit that learns to be gentle in its dealings with men and God is well prepared to receive God's encouraging instruction. Some people are born with a sensitive, kind spirit, but the gentleness the Scriptures refer to is kindled and cultivated by the Holy Spirit: "The fruit of the Spirit is ... gentleness" (Galatians

5:22–23). God himself works in us that gracious tenderness that we should demonstrate to our family and circle of friends and acquaintances. Think of your home or workplace ruled by a spirit of gentleness. What a change there would be for most of us! Strife, jealousy, and power struggles would be usurped by the love of Christ. The aggressive, type A personality would still be forceful but within the restraints of God-infused gentleness.

The apostle Peter said that a gentle spirit is "of great worth in God's sight" (1 Peter 3:4). Although this passage deals with the inward beauty of wives, it is not gender exclusive. Any man or woman whose inner self is adorned with a spirit of gentleness possesses a spiritual quality prized by God. The value of gentleness to God and man is priceless.

Ask the Holy Spirit to cut and prune your personality to produce the fruit of gentleness. Cease demanding. Loathe pride. Dislodge arrogance. As you do, a genuine, true transformation of character and conduct will surprise and overtake you.

———— ❖ ————

Gentle Savior, you deal with me in loving gentleness. Show me how to extend the same goodness to others that you freely demonstrate on a moment-by-moment basis to me.

Touchstone

Gentleness: a
seasoning that turns
bad to good.

No one whose hope is in you will ever be put to shame.

PSALM 25:3

No Disappointment

———————•———————

isappointment is a common occurrence in our relationships with one another. Consistently failing to live up to
others' expectations is inevitable due to our still flawed behavior and emotions. We frequently even let ourselves down. Can
you imagine then the thrill of a relationship where disappointment does not exist, where the sting of hurt and disillusionment
is banished? Would you like to be included in that unique bond?

You already are in such fellowship with Jesus Christ. God is
never disappointed with you. Does that catch you by surprise?
Have you spent days or months or even years thinking that you
have let God down? Don't let your adversary, the Devil, take you
down that forlorn road one moment longer. While your wrong
behavior does grieve God's heart, he is not disappointed with
you. God knew everything you would say and do—and not say
and do—before the world was birthed by his word. Your lapses
into sin or just plain blunders are fully known by an omniscient
Father. But that intimate foreknowledge never diminishes God's
steadfast love for you. God's love does not rise or fall in response
to your erratic behavior. He will correct and discipline you, but
that does not mean he is dissatisfied with you. God doesn't think:
"Gee, I sure am disappointed with Charles's actions today. I
knew if I gave him this opportunity he would blow it." That is
not God's character or nature. He is for us, not against us, and
nothing can separate us from his perfect love.

The other side of the coin is great news as well. God is never
disappointed with you, and you need never be disappointed with
God. David said of his forefathers, "In you our fathers put their

trust; they trusted and you delivered them. They cried to you and were saved; in you they trusted and were not disappointed" (Psalm 22:4). I realize we often feel disappointed when our prayers aren't answered or our circumstances are contrary. But God never fails to respond to our need in his wisdom, love, and power. We may feel discouraged, but God is steadfastly faithful, committed to orchestrating all events to his glory and our good. Don't let unreliable emotions fog your view of God's goodness. It is impossible for God to disappoint the person who trusts him, for he is completely trustworthy. Overcome any feelings of disappointment with God with new affirmations of his love for you and loyal faithfulness.

Adversity, affliction, grief, suffering, and numerous other painful experiences are part of the Christian journey. But you can bypass disappointment completely with the sure knowledge that God is profoundly and permanently pleased with you and worthy of your unceasing hope and faith.

———— • ————

Loving Father, help me realize that this cloak of guilt I've been wearing is not from you. It has weighed me down and kept me from coming to you for forgiveness and restoration. I know now you accept me and are not disappointed with me.

Touchstone

You cannot
disappoint someone
who knows
everything.

Keep your servant also from willful sins.

PSALM 19:13

God's Intervention

———— • ————

$\mathcal{D}$avid was intent on revenge of the fiercest kind—murder. His request for sustenance from a wealthy shepherd whose flock had been protected by David's men had been rudely refused by their ill-tempered owner, Nabal. Although he had just spared the life of Saul, David boiled with anger when the news of Nabal's rejection reached him: "May God deal with David, be it ever so severely, if by morning I leave alive one male of all who belong to him!" Only the intervention of Nabal's wise wife, Abigail, whose words pricked David's conscience, prevented the king on the run from slaughtering Nabal and his men. Nabal eventually did die, but it was by God's hand, not David's (1 Samuel 25).

When I read this account, I am reminded of how many times God, in his goodness, has kept me from wrongdoing. I get mad and want to act in an intemperate manner. Someone else hurts my feelings and I want to retaliate. I know that what I want to do is not God's choice, but I am determined to have my way. So often, when I am tempted to act in the impetuousness of the flesh, God steps into the picture and keeps me from sin and its painful consequences. I am so grateful to God for his providential intervention in such cases. Left to my own devices, I am sure, like David, I could follow my misguided and deceived intentions.

This is nothing less than the sheer expression of a merciful God who, knowing our weaknesses, comes to our rescue when he is under no obligation to do so. Of course, God doesn't always check our wayward actions. (Later, David murdered Uriah to conceal his sin with Bathsheba. Apparently he did not learn his lesson in his close encounter with Nabal.) But he does go to great lengths to keep the person whose heart is bent toward him from making erroneous choices.

When your heart is fixed on serving and growing in Christ, God will frequently intervene to keep you on track with his purposes and plans. He may use the words of a Christian friend, the lyrics of a hymn, the words of a Christian radio or television message, or any number of avenues to steer you away from your presumption and keep you from sinning. If you just allow the Holy Spirit to speak to you through the Scriptures, even at the very moment when you don't want to read or hear what the Lord has to say, he will give you just the caution you need.

Perhaps you are set on an errant course of behavior that you know is opposed to God's will. Thus far, you have not been deterred by what you know is the truth. Like David, your common sense and sensitivity to the Spirit have been usurped by unstable emotions. Turn to God and ask him to intervene on your behalf. He, too, is willing to go the extra mile to keep you from trouble. He loves you enough to keep you from hurting yourself and others. This is how good God is.

———— • ————

Lord, you know my heart better than I do. Search it now to reveal any ill intents I may harbor. Reveal them to me so I may know, and shut the doors before me of any wrong path I may be going down.

Touchstone

Never underestimate
the keeping power
of God.

He has showed you, O man, what is good. And what does the LORD require of you? To act justly and to love mercy and to walk humbly with your God.

MICAH 6:8

Bad News, Good News

By definition, the Greek word for *gospel*—*euangelion*—means "good news." The gospel's central theme—Christ's death, burial, and resurrection—is a distinctly positive message of hope and triumph. God's goodness in redeeming humanity and providing an eternity of unending bliss in a perfect heaven is displayed throughout the Scriptures.

Have you ever wondered, however, why so many people refuse to even listen to the gospel of Christ? Just mention sin or salvation to a friend and the dialogue usually ends with a comment like, "I don't talk about religion. It's a private thing with me." If the gospel is such good news for everyone, why do most people bristle when the subject is mentioned? Why aren't folks eager to hear a message that can change their lives and destiny?

Here's the rub, I think: Before we can appreciate the fantastic benefits of the good news of Christ's salvation, we must first face the bad news about ourselves. The gospel is indeed exceedingly good; but we, apart from God, are exceedingly bad. That's not the kind of talk we like to hear. We morally measure ourselves with the behavior of others—typically those whose conduct is significantly worse than ours. Our concept of goodness is on a sliding scale. "I am a pretty good guy," we think. "I don't hurt people. I'm not a criminal. I'm on good terms with my neighbor. I am really fairly decent, in fact, better than a lot of other persons I know."

Certainly, we can do some noble things—help a sick neighbor, rear morally competent children, give financially to worthy causes—and in general lead what our culture would deem a "good life." The problem is, from God's perspective, we are spiritually dead and alienated from his presence from birth. Our value system may be respectable but our spiritual condition is what theologians term "depraved"—capable of good acts but still enemies of Christ due to our sinful state. The bad news is we can never do enough good to enter God's holy kingdom. Try as we might to be moral and upright, we are dead to God in our sin (Ephesians 2:1).

Acknowledging and dealing with our spiritual bankruptcy is the bad news we must first face before the good news of Christ's rescue and redemption from sin can be experienced. Most are unwilling to admit their plight, drop their pride, and come to Christ for forgiveness and reconciliation. But for those of us who have understood our dilemma before God, the gospel of grace and pardon is incredibly sweet and freeing. The reality of God's love and all that he has done to demonstrate that love through Christ's life, death, and resurrection is the source of our daily strength and hope. Our lives have meaning and purpose derived from an intimate relationship with the Savior.

If you have never faced the bad news about your standing before God, don't be afraid to confess your sin. God has planned and worked for eternity to personally bring you the good news of his gospel.

———— ◆ ————

Lord Jesus, I am the person described above. I've been convincing myself that I'm a "good person" by all the "things" I am doing. Now I realize that it is all for nothing if I don't have you in my life. I accept you now as my Lord and Savior and all that is truly good. Everything else I accomplish in my life I do for and through you.

Touchstone

Facing the bad
news can be
good news.

Greater love has no one than this, that he lay down his life for his friends. You are my friends.

JOHN 15:13–14

Friends

———————— • ————————

hristianity is the only religion in the world where the relationship between God and humans is one of "friends." Only hours before his death, Jesus conversed frankly with his disciples and revealed the startling new intimacy of their bond: "I no longer call you servants, because a servant does not know his master's business. Instead, I have called you friends, for everything that I learned from my Father I have made known to you" (John 15:15). Every disciple, every follower of Christ is God's friend. True, you are a servant and Jesus is Lord, but the tenor of your fellowship with the Savior is marked with all the qualities of authentic friendship.

Many people are reluctant to think of their relationship to God in this light. They are not comfortable with the terminology. I understand the hesitancy, since it took me a long time in my Christian journey to believe God really thinks of me as his friend. I knew God was holy and awesome, but the notion of being his friend was alien. The more I understood God's love for me and the removal of all barriers between us through Christ's death, however, the easier it became to accept the quite scriptural fact that I am indeed God's friend. Actually, as I began to delight in his friendship, I found myself with a heightened rather than lowered sense of reverence and devotion.

As God's friend, it's essential to know that he accepts you the way you are. He isn't waiting for you to improve a certain character trait or reach some new level of spiritual maturity. God does not overlook or condone your deficiencies—like a true friend, he wants the best for you—but he does not reject you in the growth process. God is always accessible, and you can call on him with great confidence even when your behavior is suspect.

Honesty and openness are trademarks of your friendship with God. It's okay to talk with God when you're angry or bitter. Tell him how you feel and why you feel that way. God knows your heart anyway, and transparency before him is the best tact. God is always honest with you; it is impossible for the God of truth to lie. He will correct you when necessary as well as encourage and cheer you.

Revealing the depths of your soul to God and his wise and loving response is the essence of spiritual friendship. He's there for you whenever you need him, and he would like for you, as his friend, to believe and obey him like Abraham, his friend (James 2:23).

A. W. Tozer called God the "most winsome of all beings." It is this God who has befriended you in Christ. I can gladly lay down my life—my plans, my priorities—for such a friend. He's done much more for me.

———— • ————

Dear Friend, I am so glad I have you to go to. I can share all my fears and secrets with you and you will not judge me or betray our friendship. Thank you for loving me, caring for me, saving me, and for being my friend.

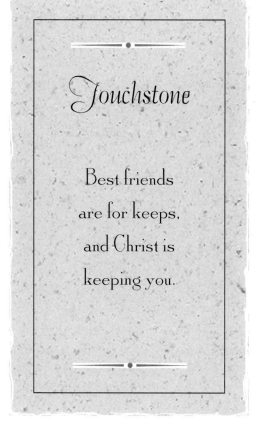

Touchstone

Best friends
are for keeps,
and Christ is
keeping you.

Every valley shall be raised up, every mountain and hill made low; . . . and the glory of the LORD will be revealed.

ISAIAH 40:4–5

Involved in It All

———— • ————

Do you need God's intervention in an extraordinary way? Do you need the God who works wonders to perform one on your behalf? If so, locate your Bible now and read the second chapter of John.

It's a wonderful story, isn't it? You can't miss the sublime subtlety of Jesus' miraculous transformation of common water into uncommonly fine wine. Full of the Spirit and leading a small cadre of disciples, Christ demonstrates his divinity in Cana after thirty years of quiet obedience in the obscurity of Nazareth. Embedded in John's rapt description of the event are several potent principles for those who long for Christ's touch of wonder today.

Expect God to act in the fabric of everyday circumstances. Jesus was in an ordinary home with friends of the family when the supernatural happened. God's most amazing feats often occur in the humdrum of the routine. God speaks the very words we desperately need to hear while we finish up the dinner dishes. The phone call with the answer we have been waiting for comes as we plow through the work on our desk.

It's essential to be about God's business in small, even seemingly insignificant matters, if we want to see him move in the more urgent areas. God wants us to seek a real relationship with him, not merely focus on what we need him to do for us.

Jesus' miracle at Cana is intriguing to me as well because it reinforces a lesson I am continually learning—God's ways are not mine. The headwaiter reacted in disbelief when he sampled the wine. "Every man serves the good wine first," he remarked to the bridegroom, but "you have kept the good wine until now" (v. 10).

God responds to our neediness in surprising ways. He may show us the solution to our financial strait is not more income but giving to him when we perceive the well is dry. In sickness, God can and does heal, but frequently his intervention comes in our spirits, not our bodies. We learn to exchange our weakness for his strength. We can almost anticipate that God will intervene in an unexpected fashion. We will know the work is his, not ours.

Perhaps the most compelling part of this narrative is the role of the servants. They did exactly what Jesus said, despite whatever reservations they must have had when asked to fill six large pots with water. Each container held twenty to thirty gallons of water, and filling them was a laborious task. But they obeyed, and when the headwaiter sipped, they alone knew someone magnificent and transcendent was in their midst.

It is the meek and humble person who sees the imprint of God's majesty in the daily round. It is the obedient disciple who takes the less traveled road of servanthood and duty who awakens one day to the miraculous. Others taste of God's goodness, but they do not know the source. The servant of Christ knows.

Will God supply the divine touch you need? Yes, but not necessarily when or how you expect. It all happens so that he might manifest "his glory" (v. 11) and so that you will be astonished at his might and mercy.

God will meet you in his greatness and goodness.

————— • —————

Father, help me to see you in all areas of my life. Forgive me when I've acted selfishly, asking for your help only when I felt I needed it. I want you involved in all areas of my life so I can witness your love and goodness in action.

Touchstone

Don't miss the
beauty of Christ
in the everyday.

Never will I leave you; never will I forsake you.

HEBREWS 13:5

Through the Battles

‫——— • ———

What do you do when you don't know what to do?
Maybe you have been there. Maybe you are there now.
Unpredictable finances. A wayward son or daughter. A debilitating illness. A major decision with no clear directive.

Jehoshaphat, the king of Judah, found himself in such a great cloud of uncertainty in 2 Chronicles 20. Surrounded by an encampment of hostile foes, Jehoshaphat faced the possible destruction of Judah. A previous military encounter had turned sour, and only God's mercy had spared him from death (2 Chronicles 18). His response to the new danger is embedded with principles that you can use in the taxing times when God seems to give no precise guidance and your logic has run its course.

Perhaps the most important thing to remember is that it is spiritually legitimate to admit your need and confess your perplexity. That is precisely what Jehoshaphat did. Speaking before a large assembly, Jehoshaphat acknowledged his helplessness: "For we have no power to face this vast army that is attacking us. We do not know what to do" (2 Chronicles 20:12).

Good King Jehoshaphat did not have even one good answer. Sometimes I think Christians feel guilty when they can't successfully work through a problem. This is a huge mistake because God often waits for us to exhaust our resources so we might rely on him. We like to think, "If I do this, then God will do that." It may work that way occasionally, but not always. God did not design us with all the answers, so humbling ourselves before him is the right thing to do when we don't know what to do.

Jehoshaphat simply called out to God. In his prior escape from enemy forces, the king was about to be killed when he "cried out, and the Lord helped him" (2 Chronicles 18:31). You don't have to say just the right words. God looks on the heart, and it is the heart's cry that moves him. Just as a child's cry brings a concerned parent rushing to help, our heartfelt prayers summon the caring Father to our aid.

When you do not know what to do, don't forget the awesome power of God. Jehoshaphat's stirring public prayer in verses 6–12 is impressive in that it recounts the might of God and his past deliverance. Our hurts can be so deep, our needs so demanding, our bodies so tired, our spirits so frayed, that we lose sight of God's greatness. The magnitude of our need does not diminish the goodness, faithfulness, and wisdom of God. When you are overwhelmed, take refuge in the unchanging character of God.

Jehoshaphat's ringing conclusion to his cry for help is vital to remember when you are at a loss for the next step to take. "Our eyes are upon you" (2 Chronicles 20:12) were the king's final words.

When you are completely baffled, trust in God with all your heart. Place the outcome squarely in his hands, tell him you will do whatever he asks, and confidently expect him to work all things together for good. Anticipate his kind intervention. Acknowledge that God is in complete control. He promises never to fail or forsake you (Hebrews 13:5).

God brought Jehoshaphat through his fear and bewilderment in the most unusual way—praise songs from a choir. He will bring you through your predicament as well, because "the battle is not yours, but God's" (2 Chronicles 20:15).

———— • ————

Father, your goodness and mercy are there in the very heat of the battle. Thank you that you are not only there for me, but you willingly take on my foes.

Touchstone

With God holding
the victory, why
let him be your
last resort?

Therefore go and make disciples of all nations, baptizing them in the name of the Father and of the Son and of the Holy Spirit.

MATTHEW 28:19

You're Included

———— • ————

*J*apanese business and industry were the leaders in developing quality control circles. Their recognition of the value of all workers participating in the production process positioned them as a leader in manufacturing efficiency and excellence. The more input the average employee has in the work flow, they discovered, the greater his level of enthusiasm and sense of accomplishment.

Thankfully, the Lord has given each believer a personal assignment in spreading the glorious gospel. After the triumph of the Resurrection, Christ left his disciples with what we term the Great Commission (Matthew 28:19–20). Jesus' followers were challenged to share the gospel with all cultures and ethnic groups, helping people understand the message of Christ's forgiveness and grow in discipleship. God could have implemented the grand work of salvation and discipleship apart from our involvement. And while God alone saves and sanctifies, he has chosen to include us in his plan.

This is why every day can be a great adventure. You are part of God's exciting plan to help men and women know and follow the Messiah. Your behavior, speech, and relationships can have a powerful influence for Christ in the lives of others. God places a high value on your participation. Though he could accomplish his purposes without you, he has chosen you to be a vital component. "You did not choose me, but I chose you and appointed you to go and bear fruit—fruit that will last" (John 15:16). Remember the thrill of being chosen to play on a team or be part of a special project at work or in the community? There's something special about being chosen, and God himself has put us in the mix to make Christ known.

Jesus transformed the disciples' small world of fishing and farming villages in Judea into a vision of the entire world when he sent them out in his name. Likewise, your world of family, friends, and work can become much larger places of significance as you are used by Christ to reach out with his love. God does have a rewarding, personal plan for you, but he also has noble plans to use your testimony as his instrument for Christ and his kingdom.

J. Hudson Taylor, the pioneer missionary to China said, "Expect great things from God; attempt great things for God." Taylor was caught up in the magnificent obsession of fulfilling the Great Commission. You don't have to be a missionary in a far land to have the same sense of satisfaction and meaning that goes beyond vocation and temporal relationships. God has sovereignly chosen you to join with him in the work of the gospel.

That's a great work, and you are part of it.

———— • ————

Lord Jesus, bring someone across my path with whom I may share your love and goodness. Prepare their heart to be receptive to you, and prepare mine so you may work through me.

Touchstone

Christ allows us
to join him in his
work so we may
share in the
reward.

Who is a God like you? ... You will tread our sins underfoot and hurl all our iniquities into the depths of the sea.

MICAH 7:18–19

Back to the Future

------ • ------

pervasive hindrance to an active, productive life of faith is a misdirected focus on the past. God is always working to help us move forward in our faith. He is future oriented. Our past experiences obviously influence our current and future actions; but when our gaze is too often fixed on the rearview mirror, we aren't going to make the progress God wants. If our minds continually churn up destructive debris from the past, enjoying today and tomorrow is a chore. The past becomes a heavy mental albatross that few can bear.

A pantheon of great characters in Scripture was chosen by God despite their checkered past. Moses spent four decades in oblivion following a heated killing. Abraham had a regrettable liaison with his maidservant. Peter turned his back on the Savior at a defining moment. Paul was the ringleader for Pharisaic persecution of the emerging church. Had they allowed their prior behavior to unduly control them, they and we would be spiritual paupers.

I'm not sure what your past holds. Others may have hurt you deeply, abusing you physically or mentally. The memories are there every day and the feelings of shame won't go away. Perhaps you are the guilty party and you are continually besieged by guilt and remorse over your actions. The past has a suffocating grip on your emotions.

The way of escape is through forgiveness—real, genuine, biblical forgiveness—that releases you from the irons of the past and releases those who hurt you. God put your sins behind you through his forgiveness the instant you trusted Christ. He holds nothing against you. You are no longer a debtor to God. You may not forget the past, but you can break away from it by extending God's forgiveness to those who wronged you and forgiving yourself as God has. If this appears too easy a solution for complex problems, it isn't. Extending God's brand of forgiveness to others or yourself takes courage and determination. But forgiveness is the only cure for the wounds of the past. Denial, suppression, or penance don't work. There is no other recourse.

Forgiveness is an act of grace, treating people with the favor of God, not as they deserve. Such grace is an expression of our faith in God's provision for our future. We can move on with our life. We can look forward to good things. We are not prisoners of our past. Forgiveness has cleaned the slate and liberated us to become what God wants. Like Paul we possess the mindset that says, "Forgetting what is behind and straining toward what is ahead, I press on toward the goal to win the prize for which God has called me heavenward in Christ Jesus" (Philippians 3:13–14). Paul's past wasn't pretty, but it didn't stop him from enjoying and serving God effectively.

Put the past behind you, where it belongs; and watch Christ propel you into future grace, anticipating the goodness of God.

———— • ————

Thank you, Father, for revealing to me how you used people with a sinful past to accomplish great things — even being a part of the earthy lineage of your Son. It comforts me and lets me realize you can do much through me.

Touchstone

Learn from the
past, but don't
drag its dregs
into the future.

Encourage one another and build each other up.

1 THESSALONIANS 5:11

The Power of Encouragement

If discouragement is the most destructive weapon in the Devil's arsenal, then encouragement is one of God's greatest expressions of goodness. The power of encouragement cannot be underestimated. Disheartened Christians on the verge of losing their focus and perspective in their struggles have been revived and strengthened through God's gift of encouragement. Sapped wills are fortified. Frayed emotions are calmed. Weary spirits are refreshed.

God encourages us through the power of his Word. Scripture is the breath of the living God. Knowing and responding to our need, the Lord sends us to a specific passage or verse to create an instant surge of hope and confidence through the helping ministry of the Holy Spirit. "For everything that was written in the past was written to teach us, so that through endurance and the encouragement of the Scriptures we might have hope" (Romans 15:4). Though it may be the last place Satan wants you to look, the Word of God is the best place to find strength and hope to press ahead. The Scriptures are so powerful that even the Son of God used them in his battle against Satan's scheme.

God encourages us through customized expressions of his grace. He gives a timely answer to a well-worn petition when we had all but abandoned hope for an answer. He surprises us by giving us the delight of our heart when we had all but stopped dreaming, numbed by the constant demands of duty and responsibility. Perhaps the sweetest manifestation of grace is the cheer or comfort from a friend or acquaintance. A note, a flower, a call, a word from a friend can put spring in our step once again and courage in our soul.

I think especially how the Lord used Barnabas in the life of Mark, who had left the apostle Paul on the first missionary journey. Paul refused to take him on the second journey; but Barnabas, seeing Mark's potential and not his problems, took him under his wings. Years later, Paul called for Mark as he faced imminent death, remarking that he was now "helpful to me in my ministry" (2 Timothy 4:11). Barnabas, whose name means "son of encouragement," had taken a fledgling young disciple and nurtured him, through a distinct ministry of encouragement, into becoming a leader of the early church. Mark's gospel is generally considered to be the first New Testament manuscript and the reference point for the other gospel writers.

God takes great pleasure in encouraging his children, as a father and mother do their children. He looks for concrete ways to demonstrate his concern. Just tell the Lord you need his encouragement, and heaven will storm your heart to show the encouraging heart of God.

I want to be a source of your encouragement, Lord. Show me someone today I can lift up with a kind word or deed. Allow me to be an instrument you can use.

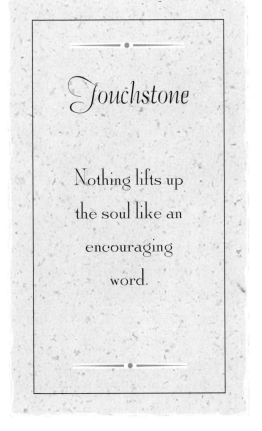

Touchstone

Nothing lifts up
the soul like an
encouraging
word.

So then, it was not you who sent me here, but God.

GENESIS 45:8

The Good, the Bad, and Our God

———— • ————

Evil exists. Bad things do happen; and they often happen to some very good people, good Christian people. Can we really cling to the belief that God is good when everything seems to be going wrong? How can a good God allow such intensity of pain or darkness of circumstance? Can't he stop it? Why doesn't he intervene?

The Bible doesn't dodge the reality of evil. Jesus bluntly admitted "in this world you will have trouble" (John 16:33). The men and women of Scripture endured adversity of almost every stripe. They didn't pretend that all was well when assaulted by calamity and distress. They asked pointed questions. David murmured as his enemies hounded him (Psalm 13:1). Job complained bitterly in the aftermath of his nightmarish loss (Job 10:1–2). Even Christ cried out forlornly in the horror of the cross (Matthew 27:46). Yet the presence of evil and suffering is always framed in the stabilizing perspective of God's goodness and power. Evil does not triumph over God's people. Cynicism or resignation is not our lot. We have been made overcomers through Christ in even the most tumultuous circumstances.

Here is the reason: "And we know that in all things God works for the good of those who love him, who have been called according to his purpose" (Romans 8:28). God acknowledges that everything is not good in the immediate sense. Cancer is bad. A son or daughter killed by a drunken driver is bad. An airplane crash is bad. There is no use trying to be sanctimonious about such things. But neither do we yield to fatalism. The Scriptures affirm that God will providentially weave our sorrow into his good plan of conforming us into the image of Christ (Romans 8:29). The goodness of God cannot be thwarted by the most treacherous events. In all things, you may give thanks because God is working for your eventual good. How? I don't know. When? I can't tell you. But I can vouch that the Lord is relentlessly and effectively fusing the harmful episodes of your life for ultimate good. Therefore, nothing is futile, nothing is hopeless.

Jerry Bridges writes in *Trusting God*: "To derive the fullest comfort and encouragement from Romans 8:28—and thus to give thanks in all circumstances—we must realize that God is at work in a preactive, not reactive, fashion. That is, God does not just respond to an adversity in our lives to make the best of a bad situation. He knows before he initiates or permits the adversity exactly how he will use it for our good. God knew exactly what he was doing before he allowed Joseph's brothers to sell him into slavery. Joseph recognized this when he said to his brothers, "So then, it was not you who sent me here, but God.... You intended to harm me, but God intended it for good" (Genesis 45:8; 50:20).

The goodness of God is the survival truth for tough times. There is no other way to make sense out of suffering. God will not only see you through your anguish, he will undeniably use it for good. Though it may seem incomprehensible in the extremity of your agony, it is his way.

———— • ————

Lord, I picked up this book because I questioned your goodness in my life. There are so many circumstances beyond my control that I am in the midst of. I am trusting you now to get me through the raging storms and show me your good will and love for me.

Touchstone

Evil cannot be

victor over a

child of God.

I will have mercy on whom I have mercy, and I will
have compassion on whom I have compassion.

ROMANS 9:15

Goodness and Severity

———— • ————

While the goodness of God is expressed in an array of temporal and eternal blessings, it is tempered by his justice. I would not trust a God who was good but not just, for God could not be true to his own nature if he did not rule as a just Sovereign. The justice of God, requiring the satisfaction of a sinless death, was accomplished at the cross. "God presented him [Christ] as a sacrifice of atonement, through faith in his blood. He did this to demonstrate his justice, because in his forbearance he had left the sins committed beforehand unpunished—he did it to demonstrate his justice at the present time, so as to be just and one who justifies those who have faith in Jesus" (Romans 3:25–26). The believer lives under the canopy of God's grace, for he has accepted the just payment of his sins through faith in Christ's death. God is his judge only in the sense of distributing or withholding rewards at God's appointed time.

The person who neglects or rejects God's justice on the cross may partake of God's beneficence on earth—rain, sun, food, natural beauty. At death, however, he will feel the full force of God's painful judgment, assigned to live eternally separated from God in hell. The great divide of hell is a severe place, full of misery, torment, and anguish of unspeakable intensity. Those who view God as a soft, compromising judge will endure his wrath forever, wrath they could avoid by accepting the love of God offered through Christ. Clearly God's justice is nothing to be toyed with since he is the ultimate ruler of mankind and all creation is accountable to him.

Still, even in this stern, holy display of absolute moral and spiritual authority, God never ceases to be good. The Cross demonstrates that the Judge of all satisfied his perfect sense of justice by executing his own Son in our stead. Those who spurn God's provision ultimately direct their lives into the one place devoid of any single thread of goodness. C. S. Lewis wrote: "There are only two kinds of people in the end: those who say to God, 'Thy will be done,' and those to whom God says, in the end, '*Thy* will be done.'"

Never make the mistake that God's innate goodness diminishes his justice. He is as much just as he is good, and for the unrepentant that justice is indeed very harsh. Neither should the believer mock the goodness of God through rebellious living. We do reap what we sow, and there are austere consequences to willful, repeated disobedience. Even so, the discipline of God, as strict as it may be, is motivated by his love and we may think of our Father as one who "disciplines us for our good, that we may share in his holiness" (Hebrews 12:10).

———— • ————

Father, sometimes I feel my faith waver whenever I see my unsaved acquaintances living a better life than I seem to be. Please forgive me for allowing those feelings to enter. I see now that the big picture holds no everlasting hope or peace for them. I lift those people up to you, Lord, that they may come to a saving knowledge of Jesus Christ.

Touchstone

The doors of hell
are locked on
the inside.

C. S. Lewis

God is our refuge and strength, an ever-present help in trouble.

PSALM 46:1

A Safe Place

———— • ————

Hard places and hard times are sure things for the believer. Our resources are taxed. Our emotional load limit is strained. The heavier the burden or more oppressive the problem, the greater our need for the strength to persevere. Rather than wilting under the weight or faltering in fear and anxiety, take heart; these are not random acts of fate, but events designed to press us to the heart of God. Perhaps the name Nahum doesn't ring a bell with you, but he was a prophet whose sharp barbs of doom were aimed at the town of Nineveh. His Hebrew name, however, means "comfort of God," and couched in his vehement prophecy is one of the most comforting verses of Scripture: "The LORD is good, a refuge in times of trouble. He cares for those who trust in him" (Nahum 1:7).

God is your refuge, your place of rest and refreshment in the thick of hardship. Unlike others who often turn us away during our time of trouble, God actually invites us to step into his safety and protection. We don't have to buckle. We don't have to panic. We don't need to look for an escape in the wrong places. We can run into the arms of God and find a hiding place where our emotions and spirits are nurtured. David's long, harrowing years of fleeing from Saul found him crying out often for God to be his stronghold, his rock, his defense, his fortress, his refuge. The young shepherd depended on God, not the rugged terrain of Israel, to shelter him. (Now is a good time to read Psalm 18.) David used the word *refuge* more than any other writer of Scripture, for his circumstances were so frequently harrowing.

Taking refuge in Christ is committing your problem to him to solve. God cares for you, enough so that he is more than willing to help you deal with your dilemmas. When you cast your cares on him, you are stepping into the shadow of the Almighty, drawing near to God. This is no guarantee that your adversity will cease, but it is a frank acknowledgment that you trust Christ to lead you, protect you, and sustain you.

We also take refuge in Christ by recalling and resting in his attributes. When your faith is smoldering, abide in the faithfulness of God. When your cleverness is depleted, ask for and expect God's wisdom. When you are exhausted and bending beneath the load, take shelter in the strength and power of Christ. When it looks as if everything is working against you, rest in the sovereignty of a God who works it all together for your good.

Taking refuge in Christ is not running away from your concerns, but coming to a place of divine perspective and power where the peace of Christ reigns.

———— • ————

No matter where I am or what I'm doing, Father, you are right beside me. You are always ready to shelter me, no matter the storm. You've never failed me in the past; I know you'll always be there.

Touchstone

You cannot see
your way through,
but God can.

I pray that you, being rooted and established in love, may
have power ... to grasp how wide and long and high and
deep is the love of Christ, and to know this love that sur-
passes knowledge—that you may be filled to the measure of all the fullness of God.

EPHESIANS 3:17–19

The Reason for His Goodness

───────── • ─────────

would like you to prepare to write down something very important. When I was in my mid–forties, I was a very frustrated Christian. I had been a believer for more than thirty years, and yet I still did not truly enjoy my fellowship with the Lord. Something was missing, and I wanted to know what was impinging on my relationship to Christ. I knew God. I talked about him a lot. I prayed daily. I read the Scriptures regularly. But there was not a divine glee in my Christian experience. Everything was a bit too mechanical.

The transformation began as I grasped the love God had for me. God loves me. As simple as that may appear, I never had understood its significance. I loved God with all my heart, but I had not fully comprehended his stupendous love for me. God began something that has not ended—revealing his bountiful love to a grateful Charles Stanley.

Now, take a pen or pencil and do an exercise that I completed. Finish the sentence below by writing in your name.

God loves _____ .

Look at that statement for a few moments. Close your eyes and say it to yourself several times. Think upon each word.

God loves you. The most magnificent Person in the universe delights in you. The Godhead—the Father, Son, and Holy Spirit—cherishes you. Immeasurably and eternally, God has set his affection on you. You are the apple of his eye, the crown of his creation.

God loves you. The love of Christ is not mere sentiment. It is infinite goodness directed to you in a myriad of ways. The love of God created you. The love of God saved you. The love of God guides you. The love of God listens to your groans and petitions. The love of God greets you each morning, sustains you each day, and watches over you every night. You are as loved now as you ever will be. Nothing you do or don't do will enlarge or diminish the love of Christ.

God loves you. The love of God is for you as a unique individual. No one knows you like God, and no one loves like God. He likes you just as you are. He relishes in customizing his love to fit your personality, tastes, and dreams. He calls you by your name and speaks to you through his Word in the most intimate way.

For the next thirty days, start and end each day with this affirmation. Rehearse it in your soul as much as you want. Maybe, like me, your eyes will be opened to the great compassion and care of God. Or perhaps you simply need a renewing touch. No condemnation. No guilt. Just unconditional, free, radical love.

May you come to know in the most meaningful way that "God's love has flooded [y]our inmost heart" (Romans 5:5 NEB).

———— ◦ ————

Dearest Father, I've learned so much about you — your goodness, your faithfulness, your unending devotion and protection. But it all comes together when I think on your true, devoted, and unconditional love you have for me. It is such a powerful revelation in my life right now. Keep me ever mindful of that love all the days of my life. Amen.

Touchstone

God loves you.

Experience God's Touch . . .

. . . with help from the popular devotional books in Charles Stanley's A Touch of His . . . series. Each book contains 31 meditations on a particular theme by Dr. Stanley, along with a Scripture passage, a personal prayer, and a "Touchstone" or personal application. In addition, each meditation is accompanied by beautiful original photography by Dr. Stanley himself, which makes these books perfect for gift-giving as well as personal reading.

Pick up your copies of these inspirational books at your favorite Christian bookstore.

A Touch of His Goodness: Meditations on God's Abundant Goodness
Hardcover 0-310-21489-0

A Touch of His Freedom: Meditations on Freedom in Christ
Hardcover 0-310-54620-6

A Touch of His Love: Meditations on Knowing and Receiving the Love of God
Hardcover 0-310-54560-9
Audio pages 0-310-54569-2

*A Touch of His Peace: Meditations on
Experiencing the Peace of God*

Hardcover 0-310-54550-1
Audio pages 0-310-54558-7

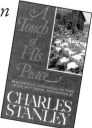

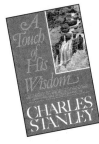

*A Touch of His Wisdom:
Meditations on the Book
of Proverbs*

Hardcover 0-310-54540-4

Also by Charles Stanley

The Blessings of Brokenness: Why God Allows Us to Go Through Hard Times

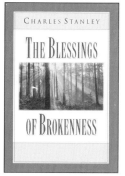

No matter how great your faith in God, pain and grief are a part of life.

Perhaps you've already experienced circumstances so shattering you may wonder today whether it's even possible to pick up the pieces. And maybe you can't. But God can—and the good news is, he wants to reassemble the shards of your life into a wholeness that only the broken can know.

With gentle wisdom, Dr. Stanley shines light on the process of being broken. He reveals the ways we protest against it. And he gives us an inspiring look beyond the pain to the promise of blessing.

"Brokenness is what God uses to replace our self-life with his desires and intents for us," says Stanley. Its end is blessing far greater than we could ever discover apart from being broken: spiritual maturity and joyous intimacy with God; greater depth and power in our ministry to others; new dimensions of freedom, strength, and peace. And a wholeness that comes as God himself reassembles us into someone more closely resembling Jesus Christ.

Hardcover 0-310-20026-1
Audio pages 0-310-29421-6

We want to hear from you. Please send your comments about this book to us in care of the address below. Thank you.

ZondervanPublishingHouse
Grand Rapids, Michigan 49530
http://www.zondervan.com